CHRISTIAN CLASSICS BIBLE STUDIES

JONATHAN EDWARDS

Renewed Heart

6 studies
for individuals
or groups
with study notes

CLASSICS

Dale & Sandy Larsen

CAROLYN NYSTROM, Series Editor

InterVarsity Press
Downers Grove, Illinois

InterVarsity Press
P.O. Box 1400, Downers Grove, IL 60515-1426
World Wide Web: www.ivpress.com
E-mail: mail@ivpress.com

InterVarsity Press® is the book-publishing division of InterVarsity Christian Fellowship/USA®, a student movement active on campus at hundreds of universities, colleges and schools of nursing in the United States of America, and a member movement of the International Fellowship of Evangelical Students. For information about local and regional activities, write Public Relations Dept., InterVarsity Christian Fellowship/USA, 6400 Schroeder Rd., P.O. Box 7895, Madison, WI 53707-7895, or visit the IVCF website at <www.ivcf.org>.

Cover and interior illustrations: Roberta Polfus

ISBN 0-8308-2088-4

Printed in the United States of America ∞

P	18	17	16	15	14	13	12	11	10	9	8	7	6	5	4	3	2	1
Y	16	15	14	13	12	11	10	09	08	07	06	05	04	03	02			

CONTENTS

Introducing Jonathan Edwards _____ 5

I THE SURRENDERED HEART _____ 15
Christ Is Sufficient
"THE EXCELLENCY OF CHRIST"
Colossians 1:15-23

II THE TRUSTING HEART _____ 22
You Can Depend on God
"GOD GLORIFIED IN MAN'S DEPENDENCE"
Ephesians 1:1-14

III THE TRAINED HEART _____ 29
Doing Our Part
"THE IMPORTANCE AND ADVANTAGE OF A
THOROUGH KNOWLEDGE OF DIVINE TRUTH"
Hebrews 5:7—6:3

IV THE WARM HEART _____ 36
Loving God
"A TREATISE CONCERNING RELIGIOUS
AFFECTIONS"
1 Peter 1:3-12

V THE PEACEFUL HEART _____ 42
Finding Inner Quiet
"THE PEACE WHICH CHRIST GIVES HIS
TRUE FOLLOWERS"
John 14:15-31

VI THE FORGIVING HEART _____ 48
Power to Forgive
"A FAREWELL SERMON"
1 Corinthians 1:1-17

How to Lead a Christian Classics Bible Study _____ 54

Study Notes _____ 55

Sources and Further Reading _____ 64

Introducing
Jonathan Edwards

O sinner! Consider the fearful danger you are in. It is a great furnace of wrath, a wide and bottomless pit, full of the fire of wrath, that you are held over in the hand of that God, whose wrath is provoked and incensed as much against you, as against many of the damned in hell. You hang by a slender thread, with the flames of divine wrath flashing about it, and ready every moment to singe it, and burn it asunder; and you have no interest in any Mediator, and nothing to lay hold of to save yourself, nothing to keep off the flames of wrath, nothing of your own, nothing that you ever have done, nothing that you can do, to induce God to spare you one moment.[1]

The ominous words echoed through the room. The listeners shrank back and squirmed in their seats. This room was not a Puritan church sanctuary, and these seats were not pews. It was a public high school classroom: junior English, American Literature. Like most students in the United States, we would not make it through high school without reading Jonathan Edwards's 1741 sermon "Sinners in the Hands of an Angry God."

---

[1]*The Works of President Edwards in Four Volumes* (New York: Leavitt & Allen, 1858), 4:318.

The class argued about Edwards's message. Some of us were Presbyterians and thought we were supposed to believe in predestination, though we weren't sure what it was. Others argued for freewill: if you wind up in hell, it's your own fault. We all agreed that we didn't like what Jonathan Edwards had to say.

The works of Jonathan Edwards will never find a home on the bestseller shelf of a Christian bookstore. They fill four volumes and require some effort to lift, let alone read and comprehend. His words can comfort and encourage, but they can also disturb and terrify. A website dedicated to his writings warns the reader, only half in jest, not to read certain of his sermons at night!

One challenge to the contemporary reader of Edwards is the dense eighteenth-century writing style. Early New England had "the highest literacy rate in the world at that time."[2] Puritan preachers assumed their hearers knew the Bible and could follow a complex argument through a labyrinth of reasoning and Scripture references.

Yet we benefit as well because to read Jonathan Edwards is to meet a flood of pure and overwhelming passion—passion for Christ, for people's souls, for godliness, for revival, for truth. Edwards's passion is always disciplined by relentless logic. He leads step by step, point by point, to a seemingly inevitable conclusion. As J. I. Packer describes the process, Edwards "uncoils a length of reasoning with a slow, smooth exactness that is almost hypnotic in its power to rivet attention on the successive folds of truth sliding out into view."[3]

Between Witchcraft and Revolution

In American colonial history, Jonathan Edwards's life (1703-1758) fits roughly halfway between the Salem witchcraft trials and the Revolution. While the Pilgrims who landed at Plymouth in 1620

[2]Allen Carden, *Puritan Christianity in America* (Grand Rapids, Mich.: Baker, 1990), p. 187.
[3]J. I. Packer, *A Quest for Godliness: The Puritan Vision of the Christian Life* (Wheaton, Ill.: Crossway, 1990), p. 314.

were Separatists from the Anglican Church, the larger wave of English immigrants who came later were Puritans who wished to reform the Anglican Church from the inside. The Church of England failed to provide a bishop for New England, leaving a vacuum in church authority in the Colonies. In 1648 Puritans and Separatists joined forces as Congregationalists. No bishop had authority over these churches; each congregation would be self-governing.

Jonathan was born into a family of Congregationalist ministers. His father, Rev. Timothy Edwards, preached at Windsor, Connecticut, for about sixty years. His mother, Esther Stoddard Edwards, was the daughter of Rev. Solomon Stoddard, who preached at Northampton, Massachusetts, for sixty years and whose autocratic style earned him the nickname "the Northampton pope." (If you sense a trend, you're right: Puritan ministers commonly spent a lifetime at one church.)

In a family of eleven children, Jonathan was the only boy and therefore the only one qualified to become a minister. His *Personal Narrative* of 1739 reveals a spiritual interest far beyond family expectations. As a boy he was deeply attracted to the duties of the Christian life:

> I used to pray five times a day in secret, and to spend much time in religious talk with other boys; and used to meet with them to pray together. I experienced I know not what kind of delight in religion. My mind was much engaged in it, and had much self–righteous pleasure; and it was my delight to abound in religious duties. I with some of my schoolmates joined together, and built a booth in a swamp, in a very retired spot, for a place of prayer. And besides, I had particular secret places of my own in the woods, where I used to retire by myself; and was from time to time much affected. My affections seemed to be lively and easily moved, and I seemed to be in my element when engaged in religious duties. And I am ready to think, many are deceived with such affections, and such a kind of delight as I then had in religion, and mistake it for grace.[4]

---

[4]*Works of President Edwards*, 1:14-15.

Jonathan entered the Collegiate School of Connecticut (later Yale) at about age twelve and graduated at the head of his class shortly before he turned seventeen. For the next two years he continued his studies in theology. During this time, according to his *Personal Narrative,* he "began to have a new kind of apprehensions and ideas of Christ, and the work of redemption, and the glorious way of salvation by him. An inward, sweet sense of these things, at times, came into my heart; and my soul was led away in pleasant views and contemplations of them." Young Jonathan explained his new experiences to his father. Afterward he wrote,

> I walked abroad alone, in a solitary place in my father's pasture, for contemplation. And as I was walking there, and looking up on the sky and clouds, there came into my mind so sweet a sense of the glorious majesty and grace of God, that I know not how to express. I seemed to see them both in a sweet conjunction; majesty and meekness joined together; it was a sweet, and gentle, and holy majesty; and also a majestic meekness; an awful sweetness; a high, and great, and holy gentleness.[5]

For about eight months Edwards preached at a Scottish Presbyterian church in New York City. During that time he "felt a burning desire to be in every thing a complete Christian." He explained in his *Personal Narrative:*

> On January 12, 1723, I made a solemn dedication of myself to God, and wrote it down; giving up myself, and all that I had to God; to be for the future, in no respect, my own; to act as one that had no right to himself, in any respect. And solemnly vowed, to take God for my whole portion and felicity; looking on nothing else, as any part of my happiness, nor acting as if it were; and his law for the constant rule of my obedience: engaging to fight with all my might, against the world, the flesh, and the devil, to the end of my life. But I have reason to be infinitely humbled, when I consider, how much I have failed, of answering my obligation.[6]

[5]Ibid., 1:16.
[6]Ibid., 1:18-19.

Edwards resumed his studies and received a master's degree from Yale. Though several congregations invited him to be their minister, he spent the next two years as a tutor at Yale. Then came the call from Northampton, Massachusetts, to assist his aging grandfather, Rev. Solomon Stoddard. Jonathan was ordained as Stoddard's associate in February 1727. In July he married Sarah Pierrepont, whom he had loved for years; they would eventually have eleven children. Stoddard's death in 1729 left Jonathan, age twenty-six, as heir to the Northampton church.

God's Sovereignty

Puritan ministers in the area met on Thursdays for "Publick Lectures" to discuss theology and hear each other preach. At one of these, in Boston on July 8, 1731, Edwards spoke on the subject "God Glorified in Man's Dependence." In his lecture he rejected covenant theology, which held that in salvation God and humanity join themselves to one another in an unbreakable agreement. For Edwards the covenant of grace was not to be made between God and humanity but between God and Christ. We then enter the covenant only through Christ.[7]

For years Edwards had struggled against the doctrine of God's sovereignty, which seemed to him "a horrible doctrine." Eventually he became so convinced of it that the subject became his constant theme. He explained in the *Personal Narrative.*

> I remember the time very well, when I seemed to be convinced, and fully satisfied, as to this sovereignty of God, and his justice in thus eternally disposing of men, according to his sovereign pleasure. But never could give an account, how, or by what means, I was thus convinced, not in the least imagining at the time, nor a long time after, that there was any extraordinary influence of God's Spirit in it; but only that now I saw further, and my reason apprehended the justice and reasonableness of it.[8]

---

[7]John E. Smith, *Jonathan Edwards: Puritan, Preacher, Philosopher* (Notre Dame, Ind.: University of Notre Dame Press, 1992), pp. 141-42.
[8]*Works of President Edwards,* 1:15.

Edwards became passionately committed to the doctrine of predestination, believing each person's eternal destiny has been fixed by God before the beginning of the world. The elect will be saved; all others will be lost. Anything less, he thought, diminished the glory of God. For Edwards, the idea that we can *choose* to accept Christ as Savior means we are at least partially responsible for our own salvation—an idea as repulsive to him as the idea that we can save ourselves by our good deeds.

The obvious question is, if Edwards held so firmly to predestination, how and why did he preach such passionate calls to repentance? If God has already decided who will be saved, what difference can preaching make? The logic of the answer is simple. Since no preacher can know who are the elect in his congregation and who are not, he has no choice but to preach as though *all* are candidates for salvation.

Edwards's Sermons

Edwards left about 1,200 sermons in writing. Many others are lost or exist only in outline form.

In the style of his father and grandfather, he began each sermon with a Scripture text and short introduction, then moved to a doctrine section, then an application section, each carefully divided into further numbered subsections. His sermons and other writings are laced with Scripture, sometimes cited by reference but more often freely quoted with no reference. To his Scripture-literate congregation the quotes were familiar.

Today Edwards would have trouble finding a pulpit, let alone a Sunday-morning television slot. By all accounts he was not an outstanding speaker. "His weak points appear to have been in voice, gesture and rhythm; his great power was in his masterful use of language."[9] The Corinthians' criticism of Paul could have been aimed at him: "His letters are weighty and forceful, but in person he is unimpressive and his speaking amounts to nothing" (2 Cor 10:10).

---

[9]Smith, *Jonathan Edwards,* p. 139.

The Spirit of God blessed the Northampton area when spiritual revival came in 1734-1735. Edwards wrote of the profound experiences of many people in *A Faithful Narrative of the Surprising Work of God in the Conversion of Many Hundred Souls in Northampton, and the Neighboring Towns and Villages.* He observed that

> the town seemed to be full of the presence of God: it was never so full of love, nor so full of joy; and yet so full of distress as it was then. There were remarkable tokens of God's presence in almost every house. It was a time of joy in families on account of salvation being brought unto them; parents rejoicing over their children as new born, and husbands over their wives, and wives over their husbands.[10]

Edwards knew that distortions and even deception may accompany genuine revival. To help discern the difference between true and false religion, he wrote a lengthy treatise on "Distinguishing Marks of a Work of the Spirit of God."

A second and even more powerful revival, which became known as the "Great Awakening," began in 1740 when the Anglican preacher George Whitefield made a six-week tour through New England. Though Edwards was intrigued by Whitefield's emotional and even terrifying manner of preaching, he retained his own subdued style. Even when he preached "Sinners in the Hands of an Angry God" in Connecticut in 1741, according to witnesses,

> he stood fixedly in the pulpit of the Enfield church, set his eyes on the bellrope at the rear, and spoke the words in a level tone and with no high pomp of rhetoric or oratory. The feelings he aroused in his audience were not of his making; indeed, he several times admonished his listeners to stop groaning and crying aloud and to be still.[11]

Leaving Northampton

Revival did not prevent conflict in Edwards's church. He was eventually voted out of the Northampton pulpit in a story which could have

---

[10]*Works of President Edwards,* 3:235.

[11]Edward H. Davidson, *Jonathan Edwards: The Narrative of a Puritan Mind* (Boston: Houghton Mifflin, 1966), p. 79.

been written yesterday. Solomon Stoddard had believed that since no person can judge the state of another's soul, no one who comes for communion or church membership should be compelled to answer questions about spiritual experience or make any profession of faith. Young Edwards went along with that at first, but after his grandfather died he reached an opposite conviction.

The issue exploded in 1744 when Edwards refused to admit an applicant for membership who would not make a profession of faith. Edwards wanted to deliver lectures on the subject. The church said no; Edwards did it anyway. The controversy simmered until a council of ministers and delegates from other churches met at Northampton in 1750.

The council found "the sentiments of the pastor and church concerning the qualifications necessary for full communion to be diametrically opposite to each other," and "not being able to find out any method wherein the pastor and brethren can unite," they passed a resolution (5 votes to 4) to recommend that "the relation between pastor and people be dissolved." The council cautioned Edwards and the church to "take proper notice of the heavy frown of divine Providence, in suffering them to be reduced to such a state as to render a separation necessary, after they have lived so long and amicably together, and been mutual blessings and comforts to each other."[12] The Northampton church overwhelmingly accepted the recommendation and voted to dismiss Edwards.

On July 1, 1750, Edwards preached a sparsely attended farewell sermon. He reminded his hearers that though a pastor and church may part, seemingly forever, they will have one more meeting before the judgment seat of Christ. On that day, he said, pastor and people will answer for how they treated one another, all true motives will be revealed, and there will be perfect justice.

Final Years
Loyal supporters of Edwards urged him to start a separate church

---

[12]*Works of President Edwards*, 1:82.

in Northampton. Instead he moved to Stockbridge, Massachusetts, to take charge of an Indian mission school. The mission turned out unsuccessful, due partly to the outbreak of the French and Indian War. But there Edwards had quietness and time to write. While at the mission he produced the lengthy theological works *Original Sin* and *Freedom of the Will* (in which he argued against free will and in favor of God's sovereignty).

The College of New Jersey at Princeton (later Princeton University) chose Edwards for its president in 1757 to succeed his own son-in-law. Smallpox was rampant in the area, so Edwards received an inoculation. Afterward, however, he got a severe fever from which he could not recover. He died on March 22, 1758. His attending physician noted his "continued, universal, calm, cheerful resignation, and patient submission to the divine will, through every stage of his disease."[13]

J. I. Packer sums up the life and ministry of Jonathan Edwards: "All his life he fed his soul on the Bible; and all his life he fed his flock on the Bible."[14] Edwards's own words from his *Personal Narrative* express the highest passions of his soul: "It has often appeared to me delightful, to be united to Christ; to have him for my head, and to be a member of his body; also to have Christ for my teacher and prophet. I very often think with sweetness, and longings, and pantings of soul, of being a little child, taking hold of Christ, to be led by him through the wilderness of this world."[15]

How to Use a Christian Classics Bible Study

Christian Classics Bible studies are designed to introduce some of the key writers, preachers and teachers who have shaped our Christian thought over the centuries. Each guide has an introduction to the life and thought of a particular writer and six study sessions. The studies each have an introduction to the particular

---

[13]Ibid., 1:51.
[14]Packer, *Quest for Godliness*, p. 310.
[15]*Works of President Edwards*, 1:21.

themes and writings in that study and the following components.

READ ————————————————————————
This is an excerpt from the original writings.

GROUP DISCUSSION OR PERSONAL REFLECTION ——————
These questions are designed to help you explore the themes
of the reading.

INTO THE WORD ——————————————————————
This includes a key Scripture to read and explore induc-
tively. The text picks up on the themes of the study session.

ALONG THE ROAD ——————————————————————
These are ideas to carry you further and deeper into the
themes of the study. Some can be used in a group session; many
are for personal use and reflection.

The study notes at the end of the guide offer further helps and
background on the study questions.

May these writings and studies enrich your life in Christ.

I
THE SURRENDERED HEART
Colossians 1:15-23

As kids, Dale and his brother Bryan ventured onto a frozen lake on old-fashioned wooden skis. They stopped to investigate what looked like an ice-fishing hole. The ice at the hole's edge was quite thin, as though the hole was in the process of freezing over. With a pocketknife Bryan chipped away at the ice edge. When he had enlarged the hole to about eighteen inches and the ice was still only half an inch thick, the two boys realized they were standing above an underwater spring. Only their seven-foot-long skis kept them from breaking through. They looked at each other and took off in opposite directions.

By contrast, ice can be surprisingly thick. We have watched stockcar races on the frozen surface of Lake Superior. The cars run on three feet of ice over thirty feet of water. They are in more danger of crashing into each other than dropping through the ice. Thick ice has produced other unique automotive sports: In Bayfield, Wisconsin, the locals used to park an old car on the ice and make bets on the date in spring when it would break through—until the Department of Natural Resources put an end to the tradition.

Safe ice or thin ice? The difference can mean life or death. Before we step out into a new situation, we want some assurance that the "ice" (whatever form the "ice" takes) is strong enough to hold our weight.

Jonathan Edwards assured his congregation that trust in Christ is far from a foolish venture onto thin ice. Christ, he said, is completely sufficient to hold us up in all circumstances and conditions. Edwards challenged his hearers to put away their fears and step out in confident faith.

 ## CHRIST IS SUFFICIENT ─────────────────────

"THE EXCELLENCY OF CHRIST" (1746)

What are you afraid of, that you dare not venture your soul upon Christ? Are you afraid that he cannot save you: that he is not strong enough to conquer the enemies of your soul? But how can you desire one stronger than the "mighty God"? as Christ is called, Isaiah 9:6. Is there need of greater than infinite strength?

Are you afraid that he will not be willing to stoop so low as to take any gracious notice of you? But then, look on him, as he stood in the ring of soldiers, exposing his blessed face to be buffeted and spit upon by them! Behold him bound, with his back uncovered to those that smote him! And behold him hanging on the cross! Do you think that he that had condescension enough to stoop to these things, and that for his crucifiers, will be unwilling to accept you if you come to him?

Or, are you afraid, that if he does accept you, that God the Father will not accept him for you? But consider, will God reject his own Son, in whom his infinite delight is, and has been, from all eternity, and who is so united to him, that if he should reject him, he would reject himself?

What is there that you can desire should be in a Savior, that is not in Christ? Or, wherein should you desire a Savior should be otherwise than Christ is? What excellency is there wanting? What is there that is great or good? What is there that is venerable or winning? What is there that is adorable or endearing? Or, what can you think of, that would be encouraging, that is not to be found in the person of Christ?

Would you have your Savior to be great and honorable, because you are not willing to be beholden to a mean person? And is not Christ a person honorable enough to be worthy that you should be dependent on him? Is he not a person high enough to be appointed to so honorable a work as your salvation?

Would you not only have a Savior of high degree, but would you have him, notwithstanding his exaltation and dignity, to be made also of low degree, that he might have experience of afflictions and trials, that he might learn by the things that he has suffered, to pity them that suffer and are tempted? And has not Christ been made low enough for you? And has he not suffered enough? Would you not only have him have experience of the afflictions you now suffer, but also of that amazing wrath that you fear hereafter, that he may know how to pity those that are in danger of it, and afraid of it? This Christ has had experience of, which experience gave him a greater sense of it, a thousand times, than you have, or any man living has.

Would you have your Savior to be one that is near to God, that so his mediation might be prevalent with him? And can you desire him to be nearer to God than Christ is, who is his only begotten Son, of the same essence with the Father? And would you not only have him near to God, but also near to you, that you may have free access to him? And would you have him nearer to you than to be in the same nature, and not only so, but united to you by a spiritual union, so close as to be fitly represented by the union of the wife to the husband, of the branch to the vine, of the member to the head; yea, so as to be looked upon as one, and called one spirit? For so he will be united to you, if you accept him.

Would you have a Savior that has given some great and extraordinary testimony of mercy and love to sinners, by something that he has done, as well as by what he says? And can you think or conceive of greater things than Christ has done? Was it not a great thing for him, who was God, to take upon him human nature; to be not only God, but man thenceforward to all eternity? But would you look upon suffering for sinners to be a yet greater testimony of love to sinners, than merely doing, though it be ever so extraordinary a thing that he has done? And would you desire that a Savior should suffer more than Christ has suffered for sinners? What is there wanting, or what would you add if you could, to make him more fit to be your Savior?

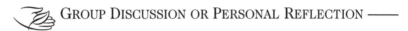 ## GROUP DISCUSSION OR PERSONAL REFLECTION ———

1. In the first three paragraphs of this excerpt, Edwards prods his listeners to identify their reservations about Jesus Christ. He counters several possible objections by urging them to consider who Christ is and what he has done. How does Edwards answer the following misgivings?

"Christ is not strong enough to save me."

"Christ won't lower himself to my level."

"Maybe Christ will accept me, but God won't."

2. Edwards then asks what qualities his listeners want in a Savior. What evidence does he offer that Christ

is great and honorable?

shares our human experience of afflictions and trials?

3. At the beginning of this excerpt Edwards asks, "What are you afraid of, that you dare not venture your soul upon Christ?" In your opinion, what fears hold people back from trusting Christ?

4. At the end Edwards asks, "What would you add if you could, to make him more fit to be your Savior?" Many people look for other "saviors," not necessarily from sin but to fill their desires or give them meaning. What are some of these false saviors?

5. What do you think these false saviors offer that Christ does not offer?

 INTO THE WORD ─────────────────────────────

6. *Read Colossians 1:15-23.* In this passage the apostle Paul names many of Christ's qualities and accomplishments. What similarities do you find between Paul's "inventory" and the above excerpt from Jonathan Edwards's sermon "The Excellency of Christ"?

7. How do Paul's words answer a person who objects, "Christ is not strong enough to save me"?

8. If someone thought, "Christ won't lower himself to my level," what reassurance does this passage give?

9. How does Paul counter the fear that "maybe Christ will accept me, but God won't"?

10. Paul says that Christ created all things "in heaven and on earth, visible and invisible" (v. 16). How does the image of Christ as Creator encourage you to place complete confidence in him?

11. Christ is not only Creator but also reconciler (v. 20, 22). What are some practical effects of his reconciliation in your own life and in the lives of others you know?

12. Verse 23 raises the only "if" in this passage. What do you find in this passage and in Jonathan Edwards's words to encourage you to meet these conditions?

ALONG THE ROAD————————————————————————

Jonathan Edwards asked, "What are you afraid of, that you dare not venture your soul upon Christ?" Venturing on Christ can take many forms. Draw two pictures to contrast "thin ice" and "safe ice." Identify some false saviors which are "thin ice." Place yourself on the "safe ice" of Christ. Use pictures or words to place various elements of your life there. (If the ice analogy does not appeal to you, use another contrast such as a broken ladder versus a good ladder or a flimsy bridge versus a strong bridge.)

Pray for courage to go ahead anyway in spite of fear. Use your drawing to visually put those areas of your life onto Christ.

The above excerpt is only a small part of Jonathan Edwards's sermon "The Excellency of Christ," in which he gives a joyous and detailed account of the ways in which Christ is supreme above all else. Of course even the full sermon cannot say it all. Make your own list of praise for "the excellency of Christ." Leave room to add more praise as you discover more "excellencies"!

II

THE TRUSTING HEART

Ephesians 1:1-14

Y ou can depend on me." Have you ever heard the words and thought, *Oh yeah?* Often you save yourself a lot of grief if you go ahead and do what needs to be done, rather than rely on an unreliable person.

Who wants to be dependent? We know a nursing home resident who was always fiercely independent. Now she must rely on others for everything, and she is fighting it every inch of the way. In our culture, which celebrates hardy individualism, dependence is a mark of weakness.

What could cause us to see dependence as desirable? Only a realistic sense of our own helplessness. We may be strong and healthy. We may be in charge of thriving businesses. We may have thousands of people who look to us for leadership. Still, in truth we are totally helpless and dependent on God our Creator and Christ our Savior.

In his first published work, preached to other ministers at a "Publick Lecture" in Boston, July 8, 1731, Edwards unashamedly preached humanity's total dependence on God. His aim was not to demean people but to glorify the God who made us and saves us.

YOU CAN DEPEND ON GOD ————————————

"GOD GLORIFIED IN MAN'S DEPENDENCE" (1731)

Man hath now a greater dependence on the grace of God than he
had before the fall. He depends on the free goodness of God for
much more than he did then: then he depended on God's goodness
for conferring the reward of perfect obedience: for God was not
obliged to promise and bestow that reward: but now we are dependent on the grace of God for much more: we stand in need of grace,
not only to bestow glory upon us, but to deliver us from hell and
eternal wrath. Under the first covenant we depended on God's goodness to give us the reward of righteousness; and so we do now. And
not only so, but we stand in need of God's free and sovereign grace
to give us that righteousness; and yet not only so, but we stand in
need of his grace to pardon our sin, and release us from the guilt
and infinite demerit of it.

And as we are dependent on the goodness of God for more now
than under the first covenant, so we are dependent on a much
greater, more free and wonderful goodness. We are now more
dependent on God's arbitrary and sovereign good pleasure. We were
in our first estate dependent on God for holiness: we had our original righteousness from him; but then holiness was not bestowed in
such a way of sovereign good pleasure as it is now. Man was created
holy, and it became God to create holy all the reasonable creatures
he created: it would have been a disparagement to the holiness of
God's nature, if he had made an intelligent creature unholy. But
now when a man is made holy, it is from mere and arbitrary grace;
God may forever deny holiness to the fallen creature if he pleases,
without any disparagement to any of his perfections.

And we are not only indeed more dependent on the grace of God,
but our dependence is much more conspicuous, because our own
insufficiency and helplessness in ourselves is much more apparent
in our fallen and undone state, than it was before we were either
sinful or miserable. We are more apparently dependent on God for

holiness, because we are first sinful, and utterly polluted, and afterwards holy: so the production of the effect is sensible, and its derivation from God more obvious. If man was ever holy and always was so, it would not be so apparent, that he had not holiness necessarily, as an inseparable qualification of human nature. So we are more apparently dependent on free grace for the favor of God, for we are first justly the objects of his displeasure and afterwards are received into favor. We are more apparently dependent on God for happiness, being first miserable, and afterwards happy. It is more apparently free and without merit in us, because we are actually without any kind of excellency to merit, if there could be any such thing as merit in creature excellency. And we are not only without any true excellency, but are full of, and wholly defiled with, that which is infinitely odious. All our good is more apparently from God, because we are first naked and wholly without any good, and afterwards enriched with all good.

 GROUP DISCUSSION OR PERSONAL REFLECTION——

1. Edwards speaks of "before the fall," "the first covenant" and "our first estate." These are all references to the state of humanity before our first rebellion against God (Genesis 3). According to Edwards, in what ways were human beings dependent on God during that time "before we were either sinful or miserable"?

2. How has sin altered humanity's dependence on the goodness of God?

3. According to Edwards, the nature of human holiness has changed since the Fall. How does he contrast holiness then and now?

4. Dependence is commonly seen as an undesirable sign of weakness. How do you think Jonathan Edwards would respond to such a view of dependence?

 INTO THE WORD ─────────────────────

5. *Read Ephesians 1:1-14.* Pay particular attention to the verbs throughout this passage. What do they indicate about God's involvement in our salvation?

6. For what purposes did God choose us (v. 4; see also vv. 11-12)?

How do you feel as you reflect on how God has chosen you?

7. No doubt Jonathan Edwards returned to this Scripture passage often; it says twice that we were chosen and predestined for salvation (vv. 4-5, 11). Verse 4 even says that God chose us "before the creation of the world." No human beings existed "before the creation of the world." Then how do you think God could have chosen us at that time?

8. Verse 5 is one of the few times in Scripture that adoption is used to express our relationship with God. What is Paul saying here by his choice of the word *adopted*?

9. How has God shared his wisdom with us (vv. 7-10)?

10. Verse 12 includes the unusual construction "that we might *be* for the praise of his glory." What meanings do you derive from that little word *be*?

11. How does God guarantee the gift of our redemption in Christ (vv. 13-14)?

12. "God Glorified in Man's Dependence" is the title of Jonathan Edwards's sermon excerpted above. Why might that be an appropriate title for this passage from Ephesians?

13. How can you bring God more glory through your dependence on him?

 ALONG THE ROAD

What are some everyday examples of total dependence? Write them out like this, as many as come to your mind:

_____ depends on _____

for _____.

_____ depends on _____

for _____.

_____ depends on _____

for _____.

How does your own dependence on God compare with these examples?

What other appropriate examples can you think of?

❷ Jonathan Edwards's sermon and the passage from Ephesians emphasize that our dependence on God is total, not simply for those areas where we need special help but for everything. Compose a prayer to express your trust in God. Use poetry, prose, song, drawing, dance or any other form of expression you wish. The prayer can include a plea for more complete trust and that the Lord will be glorified even more by your need for him.

III

THE TRAINED HEART

Hebrews 5:7—6:3

Jeremy was a gifted actor. In high school he starred in plays and dazzled audiences. We were thrilled when he agreed to take a lead role in one of our community theater productions. After Jeremy failed to show up for the first two rehearsals, we began to ask around town. We learned that all his fellow actors in high school hated him. He was a last-minute performer who did no work until the final week before opening night. Jeremy would skip all but the last few rehearsals, learn all his lines in three days, then go on and give a sparkling performance, outshining the other actors who had put in weeks of preparation. We fired Jeremy from our play and found someone who was willing to work.

Something in the gut tells us we *should* prepare diligently for an important task, no matter how natural our skills may be. Great athletes and great musicians keep practicing. They don't settle back and let themselves coast along; if they do, their abilities will slide downhill fast.

If acting, sports and music are worth diligent effort, surely our spiritual lives deserve even more diligent effort. For Jonathan Edwards, the doctrine of the sovereignty of God did not let human beings sit back and get lazy. In this sermon he reminds us that we must constantly apply ourselves to spiritual growth.

 DOING OUR PART ————————————————

"THE IMPORTANCE AND ADVANTAGE OF A THOROUGH KNOWLEDGE OF DIVINE TRUTH" (1739)

It doubtless concerns every one to endeavor to excel in the knowledge of things which pertain to his profession or principal calling. If it concerns men to excel in any thing, or in any wisdom or knowledge at all, it certainly concerns them to excel in the affairs of their main profession and work. But the calling and work of every Christian is to live to God. This is said to be his high calling, Phil. 3:14. This is the business, and, if I may so speak, the trade of a Christian, his main work, and indeed should be his only work. No business should be done by a Christian, but as it is some way or other a part of this. Therefore certainly the Christian should endeavor to be well acquainted with those things which belong to this work, that he may fulfill it, and be thoroughly furnished to it.

It becomes one who is called to be a soldier, and to go a warfare, to endeavor to excel in the art of war. It becomes one who is called to be a mariner, and to spend his life in sailing the ocean, to endeavor to excel in the art of navigation. It becomes one who professes to be a physician, and devotes himself to that work, to endeavor to excel in the knowledge of those things which pertain to the art of physic. So it becomes all such as profess to be Christians, and to devote themselves to the practice of Christianity, to endeavor to excel in the knowledge of divinity. . . .

If you apply yourselves diligently to this work, you will not want employment, when you are at leisure from your common secular business. In this way, you may find something in which you may profitably employ yourselves these long winter evenings. You will find something else to do, besides going about from house to house, spending one hour after another in unprofitable conversation, or, at best, to no other purpose but to amuse yourselves, to fill up and wear away your time. And it is to be feared that very much of the time that is spent in our winter evening visits, is spent to a much worse purpose than that which I have now mentioned. Solomon tells us, Proverbs 10:19, "That in the multitude of words, there wanteth not sin." And is not this verified in those who find little else to do for so great a part of the winter, but to go to one another's houses, and spend the time in such talk as comes next, or such as any one's present disposition happens to suggest?

Some diversion is doubtless lawful; but for Christians to spend so much of their time, so many long evenings, in no other conversation than that which tends to divert and amuse, if nothing worse, is a sinful way of spending time, and tends to poverty of soul at least, if not to outward poverty:

Proverbs 14:23, "In all labor there is profit; but the talk of the lips tendeth only to penury." Besides, when persons for so much of their time have nothing else to do but to sit, and talk, and chat in one another's chimney corners, there is great danger of falling into foolish and sinful conversation, venting their corrupt dispositions, in talking against others, expressing their jealousies and evil surmises concerning their neighbors; not considering what Christ hath said, Matthew 12:36, "Of every idle word that men shall speak, shall they give account in the day of judgment."

If you would comply with what you have heard from this doctrine, you would find something else to spend your winters in, one winter after another, besides contention, or talking about those public affairs which tend to contention. Young people might find something else to do, besides spending their time in vain company; something that would be much more profitable to themselves, as it would really turn to some good account; something, in doing which they would both be more out of the devil's way, the way of temptation, and be more in the way of duty, and of a divine blessing. And even aged people would have something to employ themselves in after they are become incapable of bodily labor. Their time, as is now often the case, would not lie heavy upon their hands, as they would, with both profit and pleasure, be engaged in searching the Scriptures, and in comparing and meditating upon the various truths which they should find there.

 GROUP DISCUSSION OR PERSONAL REFLECTION——

1. Jonathan Edwards says that "to live to God" is a Christian's "main work" and even our "only work." Yet he does not exclude other employment. How do the two forms of "work" fit together?

2. How does Edwards illustrate the Christian's need to prepare for this work?

3. What dangers does Edwards see in idle conversation and diversion?

4. When have you seen "diversions" distract Christians from living for God?

5. Edwards particularly advises the young and the old to apply themselves to the knowledge of God. Why do you think he gives these two age groups special mention?

 INTO THE WORD ─────────────────────────

6. *Read Hebrews 5:7—6:3.* By what experiences did Jesus learn obedience to his Father (vv. 7-8)?

7. What were the results of Jesus' obedience (vv. 9-10)?

8. How is Jesus' experience of learning obedience like and unlike ours?

9. The writer of Hebrews expresses disappointment in his readers in verses 11-13. What should they have been doing differently?

10. What makes the difference between the mature and the immature Christian (vv. 13-14)?

11. In what areas do you sense God calling you to start to eat "solid food" (v. 14)?

12. What means can you use to go about "training yourself to distinguish good from evil" (v. 14)?

13. As Christians we need to keep in touch with the basics of our faith. What do you believe the writer means when he urges his readers to "leave the elementary teachings about Christ and go on to maturity" (6:1-3)?

ALONG THE ROAD————————————————————

✐ At different times of your life, what have you considered your highest calling? Why and how did your ideas change over time?

✐ In journal or poetry form, write out your response to the idea that living for God is your "main work."

✐ Identify various aspects of your life that you consider your vital callings. Jot down a word or phrase to indicate each. Circle the ones for which you have a strong sense that they fit with your highest calling. Draw a squiggly line under the ones you are unsure of. Underline the ones which do not seem to fit at all with your highest calling.

Consider whether some of these aspects of your life should be changed, rethought or even eliminated so you can better fulfill your main work of living for God. Prayerfully devise an action plan to make changes as God leads you.

IV

THE WARM HEART
1 Peter 1:3-12

Amanda, a teenager, was fed up with the adults in her church. She griped to us, "During worship they just sit there. They don't get into the songs at all. They don't move their bodies or even smile. It's like they died."

Amanda was correct that her church was rather unemotional. However, she knew nothing of the other extreme, churches where the adults shout and run up and down the aisles without regard for other worshipers. If she had grown up in one of those churches, we told her, she'd be saying, "Grandma! You're embarrassing me!"

Can we judge spiritual vitality by the degree of emotion displayed? Some Christians conduct their spiritual lives according to how they feel at the moment. They need to be told, "Calm down and think things over." Then there are the folks who leave worship with the same deadpan expression they had when they came in. Amanda's words fit them perfectly: "It's like they died."

Jonathan Edwards, the supreme rationalist, found emotion inseparable from true religion. As this excerpt from his theological writing demonstrates, he was not so much interested in *how much* emotion but in the *origins* of the emotion.

 LOVING GOD ————————————————————————

"A TREATISE CONCERNING RELIGIOUS AFFECTIONS" (1746)

That religion which God requires, and will accept, does not consist in weak, dull, and lifeless wishes, raising us but a little above a state of indifference: God, in his word, greatly insists upon it, that we be good in earnest, "fervent in spirit," and our hearts vigorously engaged in religion: Rom. 12:11, "Be ye fervent in spirit, serving the Lord." Deut. 10:12, "And now, Israel, what doth the Lord thy God require of thee, but to fear the Lord thy God, to walk in all his ways, and to love him, and to serve the Lord thy God with all thy heart, and with all thy soul?" and chap. 6:4, 5, "Hear, O Israel, the Lord our God is one Lord: And thou shalt love the Lord thy God with all thy heart, and with all thy might." It is such a fervent vigorous engagedness of the heart in religion, that is the fruit of a real circumcision of the heart, or true regeneration, and that has the promises of life; Deut. 30:6, "And the Lord thy God will circumcise thine heart, and the heart of thy seed, to love the Lord thy God with all thy heart, and with all thy soul, that thou mayest live."

If we be not in good earnest in religion, and our wills and inclinations be not strongly exercised, we are nothing. The things of religion are so great, that there can be no suitableness in the exercises of our hearts, to their nature and importance, unless they be lively and powerful. In nothing is vigor in the actings of our inclinations so requisite, as in religion; and in nothing is lukewarmness so odious. True religion is evermore a powerful thing; and the power of it appears, in the first place in the inward exercises of it in the heart, where is the principal and original seat of it. Hence true religion is called the *power of godliness,* in distinction from the external appearances of it, that are the *form* of it, 2 Tim. 3:5: "Having a form of godliness, but denying the power of it." The Spirit of God, in those that have sound and solid religion, is a spirit of powerful holy affection; and therefore, God is said "to have given the Spirit of power, and of love, and of a sound mind," 2 Tim. 1:7. And such, when they receive the Spirit of

God, in his sanctifying and saving influences, are said to be "baptized
with the Holy Ghost, and with fire;" by reason of the power and fervor of those exercises the Spirit of God excites in their hearts,
whereby their hearts, when grace is in exercise, may be said to "burn
within them;" as is said of the disciples, Luke 24:32.

The business of religion is from time to time compared to those
exercises, wherein men are wont to have their hearts and strength
greatly exercised and engaged, such as running, wrestling or agoniz-
ing for a great prize or crown, and fighting with strong enemies that
seek our lives, and warring as those, that by violence take a city or
kingdom.

And though true grace has various degrees, and there are some
that are but babes in Christ, in whom the exercise of the inclination
and will, towards divine and heavenly things, is comparatively
weak; yet everyone that has the power of godliness in his heart, has
his inclinations and heart exercised towards God and divine things,
with such strength and vigor that these holy exercises do prevail in
him above all carnal or natural affections, and are effectual to over-
come them: for every true disciple of Christ "loves him above father
or mother, wife and children, brethren and sisters, houses and
lands: yea, than his own life." From hence it follows, that wherever
true religion is, there are vigorous exercises of the inclination and
will towards divine objects: but by what was said before, the vigorous, lively, and sensible exercises of the will, are no other than the
affections of the soul.

 GROUP DISCUSSION OR PERSONAL REFLECTION——

1. Edwards contrasts two types of religion. What are some distinguishing marks of each?

2. How is the Holy Spirit involved in religious fervor?

3. Where are the sources of true religious feeling?

4. Someone might conclude from Edwards's words that the most spiritually vital churches are the ones with the most exuberant and lively worship services. How do you respond to that conclusion?

5. How do you think Edwards would reconcile his unemotional preaching style with God's insistence that we be "good in earnest, fervent in spirit?"

 INTO THE WORD ————————————————————————

6. *Read 1 Peter 1:3-12.* Come up with five words or phrases that describe the mood of Peter's writing in verses 3-9.

7. Peter wrote "in this you greatly rejoice" (v. 6). What is included in "this"?

8. The readers of Peter's letter were suffering "grief in all kinds of trials" (v. 6). What did Peter expect as the outcome of their difficulties (vv. 7-9)?

9. Imagine Jonathan Edwards meeting the Christians Peter was writing to, and that he observed them living as described in verses 8-9. How do you think he would evaluate the evidence of their faith?

10. In verses 10-12 how did Peter affirm his readers' place in God's plans?

11. It is easy to look on difficulties as setbacks to faith. For a Christian, why would difficulties result in intensified praise, love and joy?

12. In your own life, when has difficulty resulted in such intensified praise, love and joy in Christ?

 ALONG THE ROAD————————————————————

Write or tell about a time when you experienced great depths of feelings about Jesus Christ. What led up to this experience? What were the results for you and others?

◯ Compose a short play, story or dialogue to demonstrate the difference between genuine religious enthusiasm and phony "pasted-on" religious enthusiasm.

◯ God has made all of us with varying emotional temperaments. Some people are easily moved to deep feelings while others are unemotional. Some are naturally upbeat and exuberant while others tend to be melancholy. Some people are quiet while others are very vocal. All can be sincere Christians. How would you describe your own emotional temperament?

◯ Jonathan Edwards did not call on his hearers to display a certain *amount* of emotion. His concern was the *focus* of emotion. He called on believers to allow themselves to feel deeply about God and be sincerely moved from the heart. If you tend to avoid such emotions, what will you do this week to help increase your feelings of love and commitment to Christ? The warmth of heart comes from the Spirit of God, but we can cooperate with the Spirit by giving him more opportunities to work. Consider an intense time of prayer including confession of sin, attendance at a special worship service or concert, listening to powerful music or spoken messages or taking time to recall the goodness of God in your life. Some will find it helpful to get alone while others will need the stimulation of a group of believers to spur their emotions.

V

THE PEACEFUL HEART

John 14:15-31

*C*ookie commercials, at least those aimed at adults, promise special times of peace. You will have a quiet moment if you eat a quiet (soft) cookie. You will shut out the demanding voices of work and children if you savor a gourmet cookie. Unfortunately the cookie is soon gone, the moment passes and the noisy world returns. No wonder most of us can't stop with just one cookie!

We all have ways to grab a moment of peace. Maybe we eat a cookie. Maybe we lock ourselves in the bathroom. Maybe we pick up a favorite magazine. Maybe we do all three at once! The problem is that our peaceful escapes are temporary. What we need is peace that lasts.

From a distance of two and a half centuries, the times of Jonathan Edwards can appear simple and quiet. The reality was more complex. Puritan settlers, especially in western Massachusetts, lived on the edge of a little-known wilderness. They were never far from the threats of famine, Indian attacks, harsh winters and disease. Their families, communities and churches had conflicts as ours have. As the following sermon reflects, Edwards and his hearers were as much in need of Christ's peace as we are today.

FINDING INNER QUIET

"THE PEACE WHICH CHRIST GIVES HIS TRUE FOLLOWERS"
(AUGUST 1750)

I invite you now to a better portion. There are better things provided for the sinful miserable children of men. There is a surer
comfort and more durable peace: comfort that you may enjoy in a
state of safety and on a sure foundation: a peace and rest that you
may enjoy with reason, and with your eyes open; having all your
sins forgiven, your greatest and most aggravated transgressions
blotted out as a cloud, and buried as in the depths of the sea, that
they may never be found more; and being not only forgiven, but
accepted to favor; being the objects of God's complacence and
delight; being taken into God's family and made his children; and
having good evidence that your names were written on the heart of
Christ before the world was made, and that you have an interest in
that covenant of grace that is well ordered in all things and sure;
wherein is promised no less than life and immortality, an inheri-
tance incorruptible and undefiled, a crown of glory that fades not
away; being in such circumstances, that nothing shall be able to
prevent your being happy to all eternity; having for the foundation
of your hope, that love of God which is from eternity unto eternity;
and his promise and oath, and his omnipotent power, things infinitely firmer than mountains of brass. The mountains shall depart,
and the hills be removed, yea, the heavens shall vanish away like
smoke, and the earth shall wax old like a garment, yet these things
will never be abolished.

In such a state as this you will have a foundation of peace and
rest through all changes, and in times of the greatest uproar and
outward calamity be defended from all storms, and dwell above the
floods, Ps. 32:6, 7; and you shall be at peace with every thing, and
God will make all his creatures throughout all parts of his domin-
ion, to befriend you, Job 5:19, 24. You need not be afraid of any
thing that your enemies can do unto you, Ps. 3:5, 6. Those things
that now are most terrible to you, viz., death, judgment, and eter-

nity, will then be most comfortable, the most sweet and pleasant objects of your contemplation, at least there will be reason that they should be so. Hearken therefore to the friendly counsel that is given you this day, turn your feet into the way of peace, forsake the foolish and live; forsake those things which are no other than the devil's baits, and seek after this excellent peace and rest of Jesus Christ, that peace of God which passeth all understanding. Taste and see; never was any disappointed that made a trial. Prov. 24:13, 14. You will not only find those spiritual comforts that Christ offers you to be of a surpassing sweetness for the present, but they will be to your soul as the dawning light that shines more and more to the perfect day; and the issue of all will be your arrival in heaven, that land of rest, those regions of everlasting joy, where your peace and happiness will be perfect, without the least mixture of trouble or affliction, and never be interrupted nor have an end.

 GROUP DISCUSSION OR PERSONAL REFLECTION——

1. Edwards speaks of peace that Christians "may enjoy with reason, and with your eyes open." What reasons does he offer as the foundation for this peace?

2. What are some sources of "peace" which people seek with "eyes shut," that is, in self-deception?

3. Edwards uses three momentous words in a row: *death, judg-*

ment, eternity. How can he dare to say that these three will become "the most sweet and pleasant objects of your contemplation"?

4. When Jonathan Edwards preached this sermon, he had recently been dismissed from his church after a lengthy and painful conflict (see the introduction to this guide). What further light does that history shed on his message?

5. How does the hope of heaven give peace?

 INTO THE WORD ───────────────────────────

6. *Read John 14:15-31.* In John 13 Jesus washed the disciples' feet. Judas the betrayer had already left the room (Jn 13:30), but Jesus continued to talk with the disciples about the series of events that would lead to his crucifixion. How does he reassure his disciples in 14:15-21?

7. What are the conditions of Jesus' promises to his disciples (vv. 15, 21)?

8. In what ways will the Counselor, the Holy Spirit, make believers different from unbelievers (vv. 16-17, 19, 23-24)?

9. Why would the disciples especially need the promise of verse 26?

10. What is unique about the peace which Jesus offers (v. 27)?

11. The disciples would naturally be unsettled by the news that Jesus was about to leave them. How does he further prepare them for his departure in verses 28-31?

12. Which of Jesus' words in this passage especially lend you peace?

 ALONG THE ROAD————————————————————

How do you respond to Jesus' words "Do not let your hearts be troubled and do not be afraid" (John 14:27)? Perhaps you think, *That's easy to say but hard to do!* Every day we meet plenty of things that can trouble our hearts and make us afraid. What are some things that chronically trouble or frighten you?

Imagine each of those troubling or frightening circumstances on its way to meet you. Then imagine that circumstance meeting up with Jesus before it meets you. What changes about that circumstance? about you?

Write about a situation in which you observed someone with "the peace which Christ gives his true followers" or experienced that peace yourself.

Pray for peace in those areas of life where you need peace. Select an object to carry with you or put in a conspicuous place in your home, workplace or car to remind you to call on the peace of Christ.

VI

THE FORGIVING HEART
1 Corinthians 1:1-17

*T*he first time we witness a severe church conflict most of us respond with shock and disappointment. The next time we see it we may wonder if we attract these situations or if they are even our fault. After seeing a number of church conflicts and hearing and reading about many similar fights, we admit that conflict is a chronic element of church life. Why? Because it is a chronic element of human life. Religion does not change that. Christians may even be more prone to conflict because we are so sure we have God on our side.

Given the sad fact that conflict happens in church, what do we do about it? Some congregations split and go their separate ways. Some bury the core issues and gloss over the conflict—until it erupts again. Thank God that some churches find their way through to forgiveness. By their examples they nullify the world's charge that Christians are hypocrites. They demonstrate the power of the love of Christ.

For all his influence, Jonathan Edwards could not prevent conflict in his own church. Edwards, never one to compromise, held absolute views on several issues. Unless his congregation was completely passive, conflict was bound to happen. In his "Farewell Sermon" preached in Northampton, Massachusetts, after the church voted to dismiss him, Edwards did manage to get in the last word about the repercussions of church conflict.

 ## POWER TO FORGIVE —————————————————

"A FAREWELL SERMON" (JULY 1, 1750)

As you would seek the future prosperity of this society, it is of vast importance that you should avoid contention.

A contentious people will be a miserable people. The contentions which have been among you, since I first became your pastor, have been one of the greatest burdens I have labored under in the course of my ministry: not only the contentions you have had with me, but those which you have had with one another, about your lands and other concerns. Because I knew that contention, heat of spirit, evil speaking, and things of the like nature, were directly contrary to the spirit of Christianity, and did, in a peculiar manner, tend to drive away God's Spirit from a people, and to render all means of grace ineffectual, as well as to destroy a people's outward comfort and welfare.

Let me therefore earnestly exhort you, as you would seek your own future good hereafter, to watch against a contentious spirit. "If you would see good days, seek peace, and ensue it," 1 Peter 3:10, 11. Let the contention, which has lately been about the terms of Christian communion, as it has been the greatest of your contentions, so be the last of them. I would, now I am preaching my farewell sermon, say to you, as the Apostle to the Corinthians, 2 Cor. 13: 11, 12: "Finally, brethren, farewell. Be perfect: be of one mind: live in peace; and the God of love and peace shall be with you."

And here I would particularly advise those that have adhered to me in the late controversy, to watch over their spirits, and avoid all bitterness towards others. Your temptations are, in some respects, the greatest; because what has been lately done is grievous to you. But however wrong you may think others have done, maintain, with great diligence and watchfulness, a Christian meekness and sedateness of spirit; and labor, in this respect, to excel others who are of the contrary part. And this will be the best victory: for "he that rules his spirit, is better than he that takes a city." Therefore let nothing be done through strife or vain-glory. Indulge no revengeful spirit in any wise; but watch and pray against it; and, by all means in your power, seek the prosperity of the town: and never think you behave yourselves as becomes Christians, but when you sincerely, sensibly, and fervently love all men, of whatever party or opinion, and whether friendly or unkind, just or injurious, to you or your friends, or to the cause and kingdom of Christ. . . .

Having briefly mentioned these important articles of advice, nothing remains, but that I now take my leave of you, and bid you all farewell; wishing and praying for your best prosperity. I would now commend your immortal souls to Him, who formerly committed them to me, expecting the day, when I must meet you again before Him, who is the Judge of quick and dead. I desire that I may never forget this people, who have been so long my special charge, and that I may never cease fervently to pray for your prosperity. May God bless you with a faithful pastor, one that is well acquainted with his mind and will, thoroughly warning sinners, wisely and skillfully searching professors, and conducting you in the way to eternal blessedness. May you have truly a burning and shining light set up in this candlestick; and may you, not only for a season, but during his whole life, and that a long life, be willing to rejoice in his light.

And let me be remembered in the prayers of all God's people that are of a calm spirit, and are peaceable and faithful in Israel, of whatever opinion they may be with respect to terms of church communion.

And let us all remember, and never forget our future solemn meeting on that great day of the Lord; the day of infallible decision, and of the everlasting and unalterable sentence. AMEN.

GROUP DISCUSSION OR PERSONAL REFLECTION——

1. Other than personal pain, why did the conflicts in Edwards's church cause him so much grief?

2. Edwards noted that some in the congregation had taken his side in the controversy. What particular spiritual dangers did he foresee for his supporters?

3. Why do you think such dangers are so prevalent in church conflicts (and their aftermath)?

4. How did Edwards advise his supporters to counter these dangers?

5. What hopes did Edwards express for the church?

INTO THE WORD ───────────────────────

6. *Read 1 Corinthians 1:1-17.* In what spirit does Paul greet the Christians in Corinth (vv. 1-9)?

7. How does he affirm their relationship with God (vv. 1-9)?

8. What conflict threatened the Corinthians' fellowship (vv. 10-12)?

9. Some of the Corinthian Christians declared their exclusive loyalty to Paul (v. 12). How did Paul put the lid on their potentially explosive allegiance to him (vv. 13-17)?

10. What similarities do you find between Paul's advice to the Corinthians (vv. 10-17) and the advice Jonathan Edwards gave his church in his farewell sermon?

11. Where does your church (or other Christian fellowship) need to take the advice of Paul and Jonathan Edwards to heart and put it into action?

12. Where do you personally need to take their advice to heart and put it into action?

 ALONG THE ROAD——————————————————————

❧ Perhaps for you this discussion of church conflict has come too close to home. If you are in the middle of such a conflict or have one in recent painful memory (or even distant painful memory), write out your feelings about it. (If you have not experienced church conflict, identify other conflicts where today's Scripture and sermon excerpt apply for you.) Identify people toward whom you have what Edwards called a "revengeful spirit." Identify any side-taking that happened or is happening in the conflict.

❧ Imagine that Paul wrote 1 Corinthians 1:1-17 directly to you. What new perspective does it give you on your particular situation of conflict?

❧ Who do you need to forgive? Write out a letter of forgiveness for that person or people. Pray for clear guidance about whether the letter should be sent. If sending it is not appropriate, you may wish to quietly burn it as a symbol of surrendering bitterness and calling off the party spirit in your heart. If you are not yet ready to forgive, express your honest feelings to the Lord. Ask him to continue to work in your heart to bring you to the point of forgiveness.

How to Lead a Christian Classics Bible Study

If you are leading a small group discussion using this series, we have good news for you: you do not need to be an expert on Christian history. We have provided the information you need about the historical background in the introduction to each study. Reading more of the original work of these writers will be helpful but is not necessary. We have set each reading in context within the introductions to each study. Further background and helps are found in the study notes to each session as well. And a bibliography is provided at the end of each guide.

In leading the Bible study portion of each study you will be helped by a resource like *Leading Bible Discussions* in our LifeGuide® Bible Study series as well as books dealing with small group dynamics like *The Big Book on Small Groups*. But, once again, you do not need to be an expert on the Bible. The Bible studies are designed to follow the flow of the passage from observation to interpretation to application. You may feel that the studies lead themselves! The study notes at the back will help you through the tough spots.

What Is Your Job as a Leader?

☐ To pray that God will be at work in your heart and mind as well as in the hearts and minds of the group members.

☐ To thoroughly read all of the studies, Scripture texts and all of the helps in this guide before the study.

☐ To help people to feel comfortable as they arrive and to encourage everyone to participate in the discussion.

☐ To encourage group members to apply what they are learning in the study session and by using the "Along the Road" sections between sessions.

Study Notes

Study One. The Surrendered Heart. Colossians 1:15-23.
Purpose: To encourage us to put aside misgivings and trust Christ because he is completely trustworthy.

Question 1. "Christ is not strong enough to save me." Edwards appeals to Isaiah 9:6, a prophecy of the coming of Christ. There, among other titles, Christ is called "Mighty God." No one could ask for a Savior stronger than God himself.

"Christ won't lower himself to my level." Christ submitted himself to mockery, beatings and even death on a cross. God himself willingly stooped to the lowest level for us.

"Maybe Christ will accept me, but God won't." God will not reject the wishes of his own Son. Their purposes are one and the same.

Question 2. *Great and honorable.* Edwards finds it self-evident that Christ is great and honorable because God entrusted him with the work of salvation.

Shares our human experience of afflictions and trials. Christ has experienced not only every human trial imaginable, but also "that amazing wrath that you fear hereafter"—a reference to Christ bearing the full penalty of our sin.

Close to God and close to us. Christ is the only Son of God, "of the same essence with the Father." At the same time, he has taken on our human nature. Even more, he has a spiritual union with believers. For this union Edwards draws on three scriptural analogies: marriage (Eph 6:22-33), vine and branches (Jn 15:1-8) and head of the body (Eph 4:15-16).

Shows love to sinners. Christ, who is God, took on our humanity and suffered for our sins. There can be no greater "testimony of mercy and love to sinners."

Question 3. Contemporary doubters may feel some of the fears Edwards names. For example, people with an overwhelming sense of sin and guilt may fear that Christ is not strong enough to save them or does not think them worth saving. On the other hand, those who think they are already good enough will hardly be bothered with such questions. Today some common misgivings are "How much freedom will I have to give up?" and "How do I know Christianity isn't a sham?"

Question 4. There are plenty of false religious gurus around. They offer a substitute salvation which ignores, excuses or even glorifies sin. Where the Christian claim of truth is rejected, people borrow from numerous religions to create a do-it-yourself "Religion of Me." Other false saviors have nothing to do with spirituality. The search for meaning leads to obsessive pursuits of just about anything: entertainment, money, sex, power, security and status are only a few possibilities.

Question 5. Some false saviors, such as obsessive recreation, promise us that we will only get and not be required to give—certainly not to give up ourselves totally. Other false saviors, such as obsessive work, demand total commitment but promise to elevate us above others.

Question 6. Both speak of the fact that Christ is supreme over everything, is the same as God and has infinite power. Both mention his physical suffering and death. Both emphasize that Christ reconciles us with God.

Question 7. Christ created everything and holds everything together (v. 16), has supremacy in everything (v. 18) and has all the fulness of God (v. 19).

Question 8. Crucifixion (v. 20) was a shameful death even for a guilty criminal. For the innocent Son of God it was unimaginably demeaning. Jesus submitted to the shame not for himself but for us (v. 22).

Question 9. The purposes of God the Father and of Christ are the same. All of God is in Christ (v. 19) and God has reconciled us to himself through Christ (v. 22).

Question 10. Christ is not someone who comes into our lives at a late date and must take time to get to know us and our situations. He already knows us thoroughly because he made us. Here Paul agrees with John, who wrote: "Through him all things were made; without him nothing was made that has been made" (Jn 1:3). The writer of Hebrews says that God "has spoken to us by his Son, whom he appointed heir of all things, and through whom he made the universe" (Heb 1:2).

Study Two. The Trusting Heart. Ephesians 1:1-14.

Purpose: To increase our sense of total dependence on God.

Question 1. Before the fall, humanity depended on God to give "the reward of perfect obedience" and "the reward of righteousness." Edwards is careful to point out that God was not obligated to give any rewards but did so out of his goodness. Although the record of humanity before the fall (Gen 1—2) does not specifically mention rewards, it shows God generously giving Adam and Eve everything they needed and more.

Question 2. Note that in this excerpt, Edwards passes over the time between the first sin and the coming of Christ to die for sin. Now we are dependent on God's goodness not only for the rewards of righteousness but for righteousness itself.

Question 3. We were originally created holy because "it became God to create holy all the reasonable creatures he created." By sinning we lost that original holiness. God gives it back only because of his "mere and arbitrary grace." Since we had holiness once and forfeited it by sin, our dependence on God for holiness now is much more obvious.

Question 5. The vigorous verbs in this passage reveal that God acts generously on our behalf (shown in words such as *blessed, freely given, lavished*) and that God acts with definite intent (shown in words such as *chose, predestined, adopted, purposed*).

Question 6. God's reasons for choosing us focus on him, not on us. We were chosen, not in order to prove we are superior to someone else, but to be holy and blameless before him (v. 4) and to live for the praise of his glory (v. 12).

Question 7. If God knows everything and is all-powerful, then he not only knows in advance who will be saved but can (if he wants) choose to save some and exclude others. Most Christians have no problem with God's foreknowledge but object to the idea that God decides in advance *not* to save certain people.

Jonathan Edwards held to an extreme view of predestination. It is interesting that at about the same time as the Great Awakening in America, the Wesleyan revival in Britain emphasized freewill.

In this passage from Ephesians, Paul's focus is the glory of God. No matter how passionately Christians argue freewill and determinism, ultimately we all agree that salvation is a gift from God and he deserves the glory for it.

Concerning predestination in another text (Rom 8:29) John Stott wrote, "Clearly, then, a decision is involved in the process of becoming a Christian, but it is God's decision before it can be ours. This is not to deny that we 'decided for Christ,' and freely, but to affirm that we did so only because he had first 'decided for us'" (John Stott, *Romans: God's Good News for the World* [Downers Grove, Ill.: InterVarsity Press, 1994], p. 249).

Question 8. Since Paul is addressing all the Christians at Ephesus (v. 1), the term *sons* clearly includes women and men. The concept of adoption occurs only a few times in the New Testament but is an important picture of our changed relationship with God in Christ. Because of sin, we are not naturally children of God; in his grace he gives us "the right to become children of God" (Jn 1:12). "Our adoption as sons is here a measure of the greatness of God's love, and is through Jesus Christ, and the strict meaning of an unmerited, genuine adoption therefore fits the context well" (C. F. D. Moule, "Adoption," *Interpreter's Dictionary of the Bible* [Nashville: Abingdon, 1962], 1:49).

Question 10. We would rather Paul had written "that we might be [busy or moral or good citizens or regular churchgoers] for the praise of his glory." The idea here is not what we do to glorify God, but what we are: examples of the greatness of God's generosity and grace. Our redeemed persons reveal his glory as a great work of art reveals the genius of the artist.

Question 11. "A wax seal would have a mark of ownership or identification stamped in it, identifying who was attesting what was inside the container that had been sealed. Because it was commonly understood that the Spirit would be made especially available in the time of the end, Paul here speaks of the Spirit as a 'deposit' (NIV)—a term used in ancient business documents to mean a 'down payment.' Those who had tasted the Spirit had begun to taste the life of the future world that God had promised his people" (Craig S. Keener, *The IVP Bible Background Commentary: New Testament* [Downers Grove, Ill.: InterVarsity Press, 1993], p. 542).

Question 13. The "glory" will include your own praise toward him and your testimony about him to others.

Study Three. The Trained Heart. Hebrews 5:7—6:3.

Purpose: To leave behind immaturity and apply ourselves diligently to the knowledge of God.

Question 1. Note that Edwards said, "No business should be done by a Christian, but as it is some way or other a part of this [to live to God]." For a Christian, secular work should be an avenue to honor and serve God. All work, whether for pay or not, whether out in the world or at home, should help fulfill our higher goal of living for God.

Question 6. "The obedience Jesus learned was the obedience of suffering. It is one thing to obey when there is no resistance; it is another thing to obey when that very obedience will bring you pain. Before the Incarnation who resisted the Son? Only in his life on earth did he suffer for his obedience. In other words, there are some things that even God can experience only by becoming a human being with all of our human limitations. Obedience in the face of suffering is one of them. This in turn brought Jesus to perfection, which has the sense of 'maturity' or 'fulfillment.' That is, through obedience in the face of intense suffering, Jesus was able to complete or fulfill his mission, namely to become the source or basis of eternal salvation (versus a temporal deliverance) to those who in turn obey him. This completed mission is the basis for his present high priesthood" (Walter C. Kaiser Jr., Peter H. Davids, F. F. Bruce, Manfred T. Brauch, eds., *Hard Sayings of the Bible* [Downers Grove, Ill.: InterVarsity Press, 1996], pp. 680-81).

Question 7. "When [the writer of Hebrews] says that Jesus' prayer 'to the one who could save him from death' was answered, he does not mean that Jesus was delivered from dying; he means that, having died, he was 'brought back from the dead' to live henceforth by 'the power of an indestructible life' (Heb 13:20; 7:16)" (*Hard Sayings,* p. 452).

Question 8. Jesus knew his Father's will perfectly; we have times of doubt and questions and must seek out the will of God. However, certainty of God's will did not make it easy for Jesus to do that will, particularly when he was asked to make the ultimate sacrifice of himself for our sin. We are conscious of former failures, while Jesus has no memory of sin. We are born sinful and must learn obedience. Jesus did not have to subject himself to that experience, but he willingly chose to come to earth and participate in our humanity.

Question 9. Hebrews 5:12 was Jonathan Edwards's main text for this sermon.

Question 12. The basic Christian doctrines will always be crucial. To reject them is no sign of maturity. But to return again and again to the basics

which we already know is a sign that we are "stuck" and afraid or unwilling
to go on. We do not need to be afraid to study the Bible more deeply. We
will never find any truth in Scripture that contradicts the basic doctrines of
the faith.

Study Four. The Warm Heart. 1 Peter 1:3-12.
Purpose: To examine our feelings toward Christ and increase the warmth
of our affections toward him.
Question 1. For false or insufficient religion Edwards uses strong words:
"weak, dull, lifeless, raising us but a little above a state of indifference;" "in
nothing is lukewarmness so odious." He even wrote that "we are nothing" if
we are not deeply and passionately sincere about our faith. By contrast,
religion which pleases God has the "fervent vigorous engagedness of the
heart" in ways which are "lively and powerful."
Question 2. Edwards says that the Spirit of God is "a spirit of powerful holy
affection" and quotes several Scriptures to emphasize the fact. The impli-
cation is that without the Holy Spirit, religious fervor would be either
absent or insincere.
Question 3. Edwards notes that fervor in religion is "the fruit of a real circumcision of the heart." The phrase denotes a heart that is turned to God
and on which God has acted with grace. Physical circumcision of males
was the sign of God's covenant with Abraham and his descendants (Gen
17:9-14). The Jews realized very early that the physical act of circumcision
did not guarantee a relationship with God; physical circumcision was
meant to be a sign of an inward change of heart. While they were still in the
desert after the exodus from Egypt, God told them to "circumcise your
hearts" (Deut 10:16). The prophet Jeremiah called idolatrous people to
"circumcise yourselves to the Lord, circumcise your hearts" (Jer 4:4). The
New Testament continues the image. Paul wrote that "a man is a Jew if he
is one inwardly; and circumcision is circumcision of the heart, by the
Spirit, not by the written code" (Rom 2:9).
Question 5. It is interesting that while Edwards himself was a person of
passionate conviction and love for God, those who heard him preach
reported that his manner in the pulpit was unemotional, even stiff. Observ-
ers cannot always judge others' feelings by outward display. Deep emotion
can bring exuberance or it can bring the stillness of awe. Believers may be
the best judges of their own hearts in these matters. If we neither feel nor

display *any* warmth and joy in worship, we should examine ourselves and see whether our hearts are right with God.

Question 8. "Testing could be joyous rather than grievous because these readers knew in advance the goal of the testing: when they had persevered to the end, the final deliverance would come" (Keener, *IVP Bible Background Commentary*, p. 710).

Question 9. First Peter 1:8 was Jonathan Edwards's main text for "A Treatise Concerning Religious Affections."

Question 10. Peter assured his readers that their salvation in Christ and its results—including their present persecution—were not random events or accidents of history. The prophets of centuries before had looked ahead to precisely this time and these events in the lives of these people. Peter's readers were even the envy of angels! How could anyone stay unemotional after reading that sort of news about themselves?

Question 11. For the recipients of Peter's letter, they would rejoice because their faith was proved genuine and that no matter what happened to their bodies, their souls were assured of salvation (vv. 7-9). The reasons are the same for contemporary believers. We have reason to rejoice in difficulties when they bring us closer to God. Concerning religious feelings, J. I. Packer wrote, "We must not lose sight of the fact that knowing God is an emotional relationship, as well as an intellectual and volitional one, and could not indeed be a deep relation between persons were it not so" (J. I. Packer, *Knowing God* [Downers Grove, Ill.: InterVarsity Press, 1973], p. 40).

Study Five. The Peaceful Heart. John 14:15-31.
Purpose: To appreciate and experience the peace promised by Christ.

Question 1. Edwards concentrates on forgiveness of sin and acceptance by God as the basis of our peace. Certainty of a place in God's family, eternal happiness in heaven and freedom from fear of enemies in this life all result from our reconciliation with God through the death of Christ.

Question 3. Every person has a natural fear of death. Without the instinct for self-preservation, people would probably not live very long! An atheist will look both ways before crossing the street, but a believer in God must think beyond physical death and consider what comes afterward. If we believe in God but do not know that our sins are forgiven, we will fear God's judgment. If we believe the soul is immortal, we will fear eternity apart from God. However if our sins are forgiven, though we still have the instinct of self-preservation, we know that physical death leads to the loving presence of God. Judgment has already been taken care of by Christ on the cross. Eternity will be spent in heaven where, in Edwards's words, "your peace and happiness will be perfect."

Question 7. To love and obey Jesus. The conditions fit with the title of Edwards's sermon: "The Peace Which Christ Gives His True Followers."

Question 9. For several years the disciples have lived with Jesus and have been taught directly from his own mouth. The Gospels give no indication that the disciples were writing down what Jesus said. They had no apparent reason to do so. Now he is about to leave them. How will they remember his teachings or the words of comfort or warning he gave them personally? Jesus assures them that the Spirit will continue to teach them and will bring his words to their memory.

Question 10. In the New Testament, the word *peace* carries at least three meanings: absence of strife or warfare, as in Luke 14:32; reconciliation with God, as in Romans 5:1; and inner peace, as in Romans 15:13 (see C. L. Mitton, "Peace in the NT," in *Interpreter's Dictionary of the Bible,* 3:706). Though in Christians' lives Jesus brings about all three types of peace, it is apparently the third type, inner peace, which he offers in John 14:27. The promise here is that "his followers will have tranquility, harmony and security in Jesus while still living in a troubled world (14:27; 16:33)" (T. J. Geddert, "Peace," in *Dictionary of Jesus and the Gospels,* ed. Joel B. Green, Scot McKnight, and I. Howard Marshall [Downers Grove, Ill.: InterVarsity Press, 1992], pp. 604-5).

Question 12. Depending on how comfortable you are with one another, you might follow-up by asking group members to talk more about the situations in which they need peace so that you can pray for one another.

Study Six. The Forgiving Heart. 1 Corinthians 1:1-17.

Purpose: To learn how to forgive any who have hurt us, especially in church conflict.

Question 1. He knew that conflict was deeply destructive to the church. It was "directly contrary to the spirit of Christianity" and would "tend to drive away God's Spirit from a people, and to render all means of grace ineffectual, as well as to destroy a people's outward comfort and welfare."

Question 2. The pro-Edwards faction had "lost" and the anti-Edwards faction had "won." Edwards's supporters would be tempted to bitterness because they felt they had been wronged by the other side.

Question 4. Edwards advised his supporters to avoid bitterness and vengefulness, and to love others no matter what side they took in the conflict.

Question 6. Paul's tone is positive, welcoming, thankful and complimentary. There is no hint that he has any fault to find with them. Paul's mood is not false heartiness or flattery. He truly sees the Corinthians as part of God's faithful people despite their faults.

Question 8. Here is a perfect example of what Paul in another place called *factions (party spirit)* (Gal 5:20 RSV). Various factions in the church professed loyalty to different leaders, including Paul. Apollos was an eloquent speaker (Acts 18:24—19:1). Cephas was the apostle Peter (Jn 1:42). Paul even found fault with those who professed exclusive loyalty to Christ (v. 12), no doubt because their manner was divisive.

Question 9. In other places in this letter, Paul affirmed his authority (for example 4:1, 15, 18-21). Here, in the context of the church conflict, he downplayed his own importance. Paul wanted to heal the divisions, not widen them. He did not want to hear any "pledge of allegiance to Paul" at the expense of church unity.

Question 10. Paul appealed for unity and agreement (v. 10). Edwards warned the church to "watch against a contentious spirit" and begged that the most recent contention, the "greatest of your contentions," would also be "the last of them." Paul deflected the Corinthians' allegiance to him. Edwards particularly warned his own supporters to avoid bitterness against their opponents. At the beginning of his letter, Paul praised the Corinthians and expressed hope for their future. Edwards expressed hope for the Northampton church and their future pastor at the end of his sermon.

Question 12. Johann Christoph Arnold, in his book *Seventy Times Seven,* relates several dozen stories of Christians who learned the hard way that forgiving brings peace, if not to a broken relationship then at least to the one who forgives. At the end of a story of Jewish-Palestinian conflict he writes: "Far from leaving us weak and vulnerable, forgiving empowers our lives and our work. It brings true closure to the most difficult situations, for it allows us to lay aside the riddles of retribution and human justice and to experience true peace of heart" (Johann Christoph Arnold, *Seventy Times Seven* [Farmington, Penn.: Plough, 1997], pp. 111-12).

Sources

Study One
Jonathan Edwards, *The Works of President Edwards in Four Volumes* (New York: Leavitt & Allen, 1857-1858), 4:194-5.
Study Two
Works of President Edwards, 4:171-72.
Study Three
Works of President Edwards, 4:10-12.
Study Four
Works of President Edwards, 3:5-6.
Study Five
Works of President Edwards, 4:437.
Study Six
Works of President Edwards, 1:78-79, 81.

Further Reading

Carden, Allen. *Puritan Christianity in America: Religion and Life in Seventeenth-Century Massachusetts.* Grand Rapids, Mich.: Baker, 1990.

Davidson, Edward H. *Jonathan Edwards: The Narrative of a Puritan Mind.* Boston: Houghton Mifflin, 1966.

Hatch, Nathan O., and Harry S. Stout, eds. *Jonathan Edwards and the American Experience.* New York: Oxford University Press, 1988.

Miller, Perry, ed. *The American Puritans: Their Prose and Poetry.* Garden City, N.Y.: Doubleday, 1956.

Packer, J. I. *A Quest for Godliness: The Puritan Vision of the Christian Life.* Wheaton, Ill.: Crossway, 1990. See especially chapter 19, "Jonathan Edwards and Revival," pp. 309-27.

Smith, John E. *Jonathan Edwards: Puritan, Preacher, Philosopher.* Notre Dame, Ind.: University of Notre Dame Press, 1992.

Trigsted, Mark, comp. Jonathan Edwards Page <www.Jonathan Edwards.com>. The "world's largest Edwards website" has Edwards's complete writings, information on his life and ministry, and links to other related sites.

White Jr., Ronald C., Louis B. Weeks, and Garth M. Rosell, eds. *American Christianity: A Case Approach.* Grand Rapids, Mich.: Eerdmans, 1986. See "Jonathan Edwards and the Great Awakening," pp. 19-29.